Michael Faraday

Ann Fullick

Heinemann Library
Chicago, Illinois

Designed by AMR
Originated by Ambassador Litho
Printed in Hong Kong/China

05 04 03 02 01
10 9 8 7 6 5 4 3 2 1

Library of Congress Cataloging-in-Publication Data
Fullick, Ann, 1956-
    Michael Faraday / Ann Fullick.
        p. cm. – (Groundbreakers)
    Includes bibliographical references and index.
    Summary: A biography of the nineteenth-century English scientist who explored
electricity and magnetism.
    ISBN 1-57572-375-1 (lib. bdg.)   ISBN 1-58810-995-X (pbk. bdg.)
    1. Faraday, Michael, 1791-1867—Juvenile literature. 2. Physicists—Great
Britain—Biography—Juvenile literature. [1. Faraday, Michael, 1791-1867. 2. Physicists.]
I. Title. II. Series.

QC16.F2 F85 2000
530'.092—dc21
[B]   00-024354

Acknowledgments
The Publishers would like to thank the following for permission to reproduce photographs:
Bridgeman Art Library, pp. 4, 7, 21, 24, 28, 29, 35, 36, 37, 38, 43; Robert Harding Picture
Library/Rob Francis, p. 5; Roger Scruton, p. 6; Mary Evans Picture Library, pp. 8, 10, 12, 16, 20,
22, 27, 32; Hulton Getty, pp. 9, 13, 18, 23, 31; Science Photo Library, pp. 11, 19, 33, 41, Science
Photo Library/C.D. Winters, p. 14; Robert Harding Picture Library, pp. 15, 34, 40; Science and
Society Picture Library, pp. 17; BBC, p. 25; Oxford Scientific Films, p. 26; Hulton Deutsch, p. 30;
Science Photo Library/Jean-Loup Charmet, p. 39; The Royal Mail, p. 42.

Cover photograph reproduced with permission of Hulton Getty.

Some words are shown in bold, **like this.** You can find out what
they mean by looking in the glossary.

Contents

Changing Times

In 1791, an ordinary couple in Newington, England, quietly celebrated the birth of their third child and second son. James and Margaret Faraday had only recently moved south from Yorkshire, and times were hard. No one could have imagined the impact that their new baby, named Michael, was going to have on the world.

A world of darkness

When Michael Faraday was born, King George III was on the throne of England. People still relied heavily on candles and oil lamps for their lighting, and on fires both for heating and for cooking. Steam power was used in industry, but it had not yet been harnessed as a method of transport. Cars were undreamed of.

It is hard for us, with our modern homes and schools, to imagine the lack of technology in the late eighteenth century.

By the eighteenth century, people were moving away from **alchemy** to a less mystical, more scientific examination of the world around them. Some interesting work was being done on electricity and magnetism, and scientists were beginning to wonder whether there might be a link between the two. Scientific minds and methods were becoming more rigorous and logical. The time had come for scientists such as Humphry Davy, Michael Faraday, and their contemporaries to flourish.

There has been great progress in technology since the days of Michael Faraday, but power stations like this one still rely on the dynamo he invented.

A light shines out

By the end of Michael Faraday's brilliant life, electricity and magnetism had been more than linked—they had been yoked together in the form of a **dynamo** to produce electrical power at will. The dynamo is still, to this day, at the heart of electrical power production wherever it takes place, whether in a small wind **generator** in the developing world, or in a massive power station. With this discovery and many others, Michael Faraday left an **indelible** mark on scientific history.

The Blacksmith's Son

Michael Faraday's parents got to know each other as they walked across wonderful Yorkshire countryside like this.

In 1756, Robert Faraday married Elizabeth Dean, and together they moved into Clapham Wood Hall, the home of the Dean family. This was a small farm of about 46 acres (19 hectares) in Yorkshire, in the north of England, which produced barely enough food to support the Faraday family—by 1775, there were ten children! One son became an innkeeper, one a tailor, and another a weaver. The third son, James, was **apprenticed** to a **blacksmith** as soon as he was old enough.

James and Margaret

The Faraday family was similar to many others of the time, except that the Faradays were members of a small and exclusive religious group known as the **Sandemanians.** This limited their social life and their choice of people to marry, but James was lucky. His oldest brother Richard moved to a neighboring village called Kirkby Stephen, where he became a successful businessman and married Mary Hastwell, the daughter of another Sandemanian family he had met at the small local church. He suggested James set up a blacksmith shop close by at Outhgill, and introduced him to Mary's sister, Margaret, who worked as a servant at a nearby farm. James and Margaret regularly walked to church together and home again, and a relationship developed between them. They were married on June 11, 1786.

A star is born

For the first year or two, things went well. The **smithy** prospered, and James and Margaret started a family. In 1787, they had a daughter, Elizabeth, and in 1788, Robert, their first son, was born.

Michael Faraday grew up in a small mews, far removed from the elegance of this central London setting.

But in 1789, England suffered a depression, as the dramatic events in Europe during the **French Revolution** brought trade between France and England to a halt. Worse, James Faraday's health began to fail; the strain of running his own smithy took a toll on him. Travelers stopping to have their horses' shoes replaced convinced him that he would do better in London. In 1791, the family left Yorkshire and moved into rented rooms in Newington, which was quite close to London. It was there that Michael Faraday was born, on September 22, 1791. Shortly afterwards, the family moved again, this time to cramped quarters in Jacob's Well **Mews** in the capital itself.

The Apprentice Boy

As a boy, Michael Faraday was happier playing marbles on the streets than working at school.

In Faraday's words:

Michael Faraday is said to have remarked: *"My education was of the most ordinary description, consisting of little more than the rudiments [basics] of reading, writing, and arithmetic at a common day-school. My hours out of school were passed at home and in the streets."*

Michael Faraday's childhood seems to have been poor but happy. Times were hard because his father's health continued to be bad, so the family had little money coming in. In fact, in 1801, things were so difficult that Michael often had to survive for a whole week on a single loaf of bread! There were four children in the Faraday family. Michael got along well with Elizabeth and Robert, his older sister and brother, and adored his younger sister, Margaret, who was born in 1802.

A genius at school?

Young Michael had very little formal education. He was far happier playing out on the streets.

The poverty of his childhood never seemed to affect Michael in later life, but the love and happy times he shared with his family, as well as the strict teachings of their **Sandemanian** faith, were a lifelong source of strength to him. Sandemanians believed that every word of the Bible was true, and rejected material wealth and fame. They discouraged close friendships with anyone who was not part of their small community, so it was only on Sundays, when he was surrounded by fellow believers, that Michael could truly relax and make friends.

The errand boy

When Michael Faraday was thirteen, he started work as an errand boy for Mr. Riebau, a local bookseller and bookbinder. He delivered newspapers that Mr. Riebau loaned to his customers, and then returned to collect them later! In between his journeys, he must have spent some time in the shop, and began to develop a great love of books. He made a very good impression on his employer, who was a generous and kindly man. He realized that the Faraday family would never be able to afford the apprenticeship fees for Michael and, in 1805, offered to take him on as an **apprentice** bookbinder for nothing. These were happy times for Michael. He enjoyed his work and loved reading the books he was binding.

Inspired by the science books found in Mr. Riebau's bookshop, the young Faraday began to experiment with electrical machines. Here, Mr. Riebau demonstrates one of the machines to a potential customer.

Moving On

Attending lectures given by leading scientists of the day opened up a whole new world for Michael Faraday.

Michael Faraday and his fellow **apprentices** had a very enjoyable time when they worked for Mr. Riebau the bookbinder, but none of them followed him into the profession they were training for. Faraday became a great scientist, and of his two fellow apprentices, one became a comedian and the other a professional singer! There was pleasant company in the shop, and many interesting books to read. One book called *The Improvement of the Mind* was an inspiration to him, giving structure and method to his thoughts. He also devoured science books and encyclopedias.

The City Philosophical Society

After reading some articles by a chemist named James Tytler about his work on electricity, Faraday was captivated by the subject. His brother, Robert, paid the fee for him to attend some science lectures given by John Tatum, who was a member of the **Royal Institution.** Tatum set up the City Philosophical Society at his home, to provide an opportunity for young men interested in science to meet, hear lectures, and carry out experiments. There, Faraday met a group of other like-minded young men, and exchanged ideas and letters with them on the subjects of physics and chemistry.

The Davy lectures

In 1812, Mr. Dance, a customer of Mr. Riebau and a member of the Royal Institution, was so impressed with some of Faraday's chemistry work that he gave the young man tickets for a series of four lectures to be given at the Institution by Sir Humphry Davy, the greatest scientist of the day. Captivated, Faraday made detailed lecture notes as he listened. He later illustrated and bound these notes—they would be very valuable to him in the future.

In 1812, after seven years, Faraday's apprenticeship was over, and he could no longer stay at Mr. Riebau's bookshop. Now that he was a qualified bookbinder, he got a job with a Frenchman named Mr. De La Roche, who was known for his short temper. Although Faraday was now earning some money and could help to support the family, he was very unhappy with his work. He became more and more determined to leave bookbinding and pursue a scientific career.

Handsome, dynamic, and a brilliant lecturer, Humphry Davy immediately converted Michael Faraday to his ideas on electricity.

In Faraday's words:

Faraday was constantly thinking about the world around him in a scientific way, but he also had a great sense of humor. When he wrote to his best friend Benjamin Abbott (whom he met at the City Philosophical Society), he was always poking fun at himself:

*"I set off from you at a run and did not stop until I found myself in the midst of a puddle and a **quandary** of thoughts respecting the heat generated by animal bodies by exercise…[On falling]… the **velocity** and **momentum** of falling bodies next struck not only my mind but my head, my ears, my hands, my back and various other parts of my body…"*

11

A Fortunate Fight

By the autumn of 1812, Michael Faraday was very unhappy about the direction his life was taking. Determined to leave bookbinding behind him, he wrote to Sir Joseph Banks, president of the **Royal Society,** begging to be placed in any scientific post, however lowly. But he had no response, and began to despair. In December, he wrote to Sir Humphry Davy personally, again begging for a position, and sending along the bound copy of notes he had made from Davy's lectures. Davy was flattered—but there were no vacancies at the time.

Then Faraday's first chance came. Davy injured his eye during an explosive experiment and could neither read nor write. Faraday was invited to spend a few days making neat copies of some of Davy's notes so they could be published. This brief taste of the scientific life fired Faraday's determination even more.

A lucky break

In 1813, Michael Faraday was given his second opportunity to join the ranks of the real scientists—this time in a full-time position. A laboratory assistant at the **Royal Institution** got in a fight with the man who made the instruments needed for the experiments and was fired on the spot. When Humphry Davy suggested Michael Faraday as his replacement, he was hired. In addition to his salary, he was given two rooms at the Institution, plus fuel and candles—allowing him the opportunity to move out of the family home.

Sir Joseph Banks was president of the Royal Society at the time when Faraday was struggling to find his first scientific job.

Sir Humphry Davy

Humphry Davy was one of the great scientists of his day. He was born in Cornwall, England, in 1778. After serving as an **apprentice** to a surgeon and **apothecary,** he became deeply involved in chemistry. By the time he was 23, he was assistant lecturer in chemistry and director of the laboratory at the Royal Institution; a year later, he was promoted to full professor of chemistry. He was a very active researcher and always liked to see a practical application for his discoveries. He carried out enormous amounts of work on **electrochemistry,** became a **fellow** of the Royal Society at the age of 25, and by the time he was in his early thirties, he was regarded as the best chemist of his time. Faraday was fortunate indeed to come to the attention of such a brilliant and influential man.

Michael Faraday was full of enthusiasm for science and for life when he started work at the Royal Institution as a young man.

In Davy's words:

Davy recommended the young man he had met briefly as follows: *"His name is Michael Faraday...His habits seem good, his disposition active and cheerful, and his manner intelligent."*

Faraday was delighted with his new job and threw himself into it, body and soul. Within weeks of starting out as a laboratory assistant, he was carrying out his own research and was soon a valued member of the team at the **Royal Institution.** Then, in the autumn of 1813, Humphry Davy offered him a place on his expedition to Europe, promising that his position at the Institution would still be there when they returned.

A European experience

Traveling around Europe during the breakup of the **Napoleonic Empire** could have been difficult and dangerous, but Davy's excellent reputation opened doors for them wherever they went. Not only did Faraday benefit from Davy's explanations of the science they experienced as they traveled, but he also had the opportunity to meet many of the other great physicists and chemists of the time. In France, eminent scientists met and shared ideas with the party from Britain. The French scientists showed the British a new substance they had discovered.

Davy set to work and very rapidly decided that this substance was a new **element,** similar to **chlorine.** He suggested a name for it: **iodine.** Faraday, who was fascinated to see the master chemist at work in this way, took a lot of notes and learned a great deal about scientific technique along the way.

Dark gray metallic crystals that produced a beautiful purple gas when heated—this was the strange new substance, extracted from sea algae, that the French showed Davy and his companions. Davy named it iodine.

In 1814, they entered Italy, again talking with the local scientists and taking in all the country had to offer.

The "fly in the ointment"

Faraday's enjoyment of his European trip was spoiled by just one thing—Humphry Davy's wife. Lady Davy was a chatterbox and a snob, not a very thoughtful or pleasant woman. She picked on Faraday with her sharp tongue, perhaps jealous because he was so close to her husband. At first, it simply made him homesick and unhappy, but later he decided he would no longer suffer her insults in silence, and began to retaliate. Humphry Davy himself was caught in the middle! This unpleasant atmosphere, combined with the escape of Napoleon from exile on the island of Elba, led the company to cut short their visit, and in April 1815, they hastily returned to England.

Florence was the city which really captivated Michael Faraday. He loved the climate, the architecture, and the scientific wonders, such as Galileo's telescope.

A Job at the Royal Institution

Back in England, Michael Faraday returned to the **Royal Institution,** no longer a lowly laboratory assistant. He now held the title of Assistant and Superintendent of the **Apparatus** of the Laboratory and Mineralogical Collection, and got a raise in salary to go with the new position. He was also given some better rooms at the very top of the Royal Institution, but only after a battle with the current occupant, who did not want to give them up! Faraday was delighted to be back at work and eagerly plunged into the responsibilities of his new position.

A focus on work

Faraday took his work very seriously. As well as working on research projects, he spent much time in the library, building up his knowledge and understanding of chemistry. In 1816, he published his first paper, and he also began to spread his knowledge by delivering lectures. However, he was a very modest man, and took the trouble to study lecturing techniques

Hans Christian Oersted was a Danish scientist who spent his life working on the links between electricity and magnetism.

HANS CHRISTIAN OERSTED

While working at the University of Copenhagen in Denmark, Hans Christian Oersted (1777–1851) discovered that if a compass needle was brought near to a wire that had an electric current flowing through it, the needle was affected and moved. He also found that the magnetic force created by the current was circular, surrounding the wire. In 1820, Oersted published a paper describing his findings. It was this that intrigued Michael Faraday and encouraged him to change the focus of his research.

Faraday's new electromagnetic apparatus was the first electric motor.

and styles before he began to give talks himself. Between the years 1815 and 1819, he gave lectures to the City Philosophical Society, the very group among whom he himself had first heard Mr. Tatum's lectures and been inspired. Faraday was increasingly known as a talented chemist, and people turned to him as a consultant for advice on their research. But in 1821, Faraday moved away from his beloved chemistry to try his hand at investigating **electromagnetism.**

A new direction

Oersted's discoveries stimulated scientists—or natural philosophers, as they still liked to be known—all over Europe. Davy immediately began working on the discoveries, but in his haste, he jumped to the wrong conclusions. He then teamed up with his good friend and fellow scientist William Wollaston, who developed an idea that a wire could be made to revolve around its own **axis.** He and Davy could not make this work, and discussed the difficulties with Faraday. Faraday was busy with other things at the time, but not long afterward, in 1821, he felt he could see a solution to the problem Davy and Wollaston had posed. He produced, with great ingenuity, the first ever electric motor, with a wire turning around a magnet.

Controversy!

William Hyde Wollaston had discussed ideas for an electric motor with Faraday, but a misunderstanding over publishing the results caused a rift between the two.

When Michael Faraday first set up his electric motor in 1821, he realized how much it would interest William Wollaston. He visited Wollaston's house in the hope of discussing these new ideas with him, but Wollaston was away. Instead of waiting until Wollaston returned, Faraday was so excited by his discovery that he went ahead and published his results, a decision he ended up regretting for a long time. Immediately, everyone who had known Wollaston's ideas on rotations in a magnetic field jumped to the conclusion that Faraday had stolen these ideas, added a bit to them, and then published a paper about them, without any acknowledgment of the help he had received from either Wollaston himself or from Humphry Davy.

Shamed!

Michael Faraday was deeply embarrassed and shamed by the outcry that his publication on **electromagnetism** caused. He tried very hard to explain his actions to Wollaston, who was much his senior, but Wollaston took little notice. Davy also made little effort to help his young assistant—he, too, felt resentment toward Faraday, and may have been a little jealous of his success. Relations within the **Royal Institution** became very strained, until in 1823, Faraday apologized again to both Davy and Wollaston, and returned to his chemistry. He also spent most of his time for several years investigating and developing new types of steel that were stronger and would not rust.

Chlorine chemistry

Faraday had always been fascinated by **chlorine,** a yellowish-green poisonous gas, and in the 1820s, he carried out some new investigations into the **element.** In 1823, he prepared some chlorine hydrate—chlorine combined chemically with hydrogen and oxygen—and, at Davy's suggestion, heated it in a sealed tube. He first thought that the oily yellow liquid that collected was dirt from the tube—but then realized it was liquid chlorine. Faraday went on to liquefy a number of other substances, including sulfur dioxide, carbon dioxide, and ammonia. These are not easy procedures, and a number of times the sealed tubes exploded, causing damage—fortunately temporary—to his eyes. But now Faraday created controversy once more. When he published the results of his experiments with liquefied chlorine, Sir Humphry was hurt at not being mentioned, so he attached a paragraph in which he claimed most of the credit for the discovery. Once again, Faraday fell from grace.

In Faraday's words:

Less than a week after the publication of his paper, Faraday wrote to his friend James Stodart: *"You know perfectly well what distress the unexpected reception of my paper on magnetism in public has caused me, and you will not therefore be surprised at my anxiety to get out of it…"*

When Faraday liquefied poisonous yellow chlorine, he again ran into conflict, this time with Sir Humphry Davy.

Faraday and his Faith

One of the most important factors in the life of Michael Faraday was his deep and abiding faith in the teachings of the **Sandemanian** Church. The Sandemanians were a small and exclusive religious group, or sect, that had appeared originally as a breakaway group from the Church of Scotland. Robert Sandeman, from whom the sect took its name, was the son-in-law of one of the original founders, John Glas. It was Sandeman who wrote down the teachings of the new church, based wholly on the teachings of Jesus Christ in the New Testament.

Sandemanians followed a number of principles, and Faraday stuck closely to these throughout his life. In memory of Jesus Christ's sacrifice for people, the love-feast—a "Last Supper" type of meal—and the washing of each other's feet were important rituals. Christ's kingdom, they said, is not of this world, so members of the church were discouraged from becoming wealthy and worldly. Sandemanians tried to live in imitation of the way Christ lived, but in doing this, made themselves exclusive and somewhat isolated. True friendships and marriages were allowed only within their own small community.

Faraday's work would have been impossible without Alessandro Volta, the man who invented the battery in about 1800. Here, he demonstrates his invention to Napoleon.

A change of heart

Michael Faraday was so dedicated to his work and the search for scientific truth that he had no time for thoughts of women or marriage.

One of Faraday's Sandemanian friends, Edward Barnard, gleefully told his sister Sarah about an anti-love poem Faraday had written. Whether she took this as a challenge we shall never know, but she quickly made a strong positive impression on Faraday. Michael was a good-looking and successful young man. Sarah was a warm, charming, and attractive young woman. It was not long before Faraday was pursuing her with all the energy he had previously given to his work. Fortunately, both Sarah and her family liked Michael—indeed, Sarah's feelings went well beyond mere liking! On June 12, 1821, Sarah Barnard and Michael Faraday were married. Theirs was a partnership of deep love and affection that lasted throughout their lives.

In Faraday's words:

Faraday wrote a short poem about marriage:

"What is the pest and plague of human life?

And what is the curse that often brings a wife?

'tis Love."

Sarah Barnard became Sarah Faraday, and changed Faraday's views on love and marriage forever.

Davy, inventor of the miner's safety lamp (shown here), was certainly unhappy at the prospect of Faraday becoming a fellow of the Royal Society.

By 1823, when he was still only 32, Michael Faraday had accumulated an impressive body of work. His discovery of the electric motor alone had made him an international figure, since people in many countries recognized its potential and began developing motors that could be used in different ways. However, Faraday himself showed little interest in the practical applications of his work. His patient, meticulous approach to his research marked him as a true laboratory-based scientist of the highest quality. In 1823, in recognition of his work, he was recommended for election as a **fellow** of the **Royal Society.** Then, as now, this was the greatest honor that could be given to a living scientist in Great Britain. But Faraday knew that the issue of Wollaston and the electric motor still bothered Sir Humphry Davy, who was president of the **Royal Society.** As Faraday's star was rising, Davy's was beginning to fade. In fact, Davy was probably jealous of the impact Faraday was making.

However, Faraday was elected a fellow of the Royal Society in 1824, with only one person—Davy—opposing his election!

This is the Royal Institution, where Michael Faraday carried out much of his greatest work and to which he was deeply dedicated.

The Royal Institution

Davy was too honest a man to hold a grudge against the genius of Faraday for long. As the older man's health began to deteriorate, he spent less and less time at his research in the **Royal Institution.** In 1825, Davy suggested that Faraday should be appointed director of the laboratory at the Royal Institution. This change of heart took Faraday by surprise, but he did not let Davy down. He was delighted with his new position—even though it brought him no more money—and he carried it out with unswerving dedication. He and Sarah lived in rooms at the Royal Institution, so Faraday could work late in his laboratory but still see his wife. Their family parties and celebrations became well known, and young nephews and nieces were frequent visitors to the laboratories, where they watched the great scientist and his colleagues at work.

In Faraday's words:

Years after the event, Faraday described an interview he had with Davy about the certificate which indicated his standing for election to the Royal Society: *"Sir H. Davy told me I must take down my certificate. I replied…it was put up by my proposers. He then said I must get my proposers to take it down…Then he said, 'I as president will take it down…'"*

Faraday's Functions

Michael Faraday had a gift for explaining science to others. The lecture theater was always packed to capacity—even Queen Victoria's husband, Prince Albert, and her son, the Prince of Wales, attended the Christmas lectures.

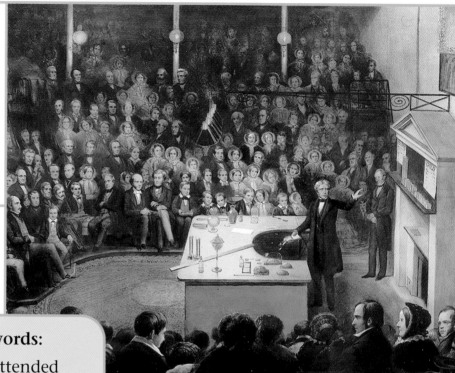

In Lady Holland's words:

Lady Holland, who attended some of Faraday's lectures, described the flavor of the evening: *"…He had his audience at his command…he had nothing to fret him, and he could give his eloquence full sway. [His]… eloquence…compelled attention and insisted on sympathy. It waked the young from their visions and the old from their dreams… His enthusiasm sometimes carried him to the point of ecstasy…his hair streamed out from his head, his hands were full of nervous action, his light, lithe body seemed to quiver with its eager life. His audience took fire with him."* Clearly, Faraday was a hugely inspirational speaker!

When Michael Faraday became director of the laboratory, he brought a breath of fresh air to the **Royal Institution.** Davy had been a brilliant lecturer in his prime, and Faraday worked hard to become a worthy successor. One of the first things he did as director was to invite members to visit the Royal Institution on certain evenings to hear of the latest research and discoveries that the scientists were making. By 1826, these meetings had been moved to a regular slot on Friday evenings during winter and spring. These Friday evening talks soon became famous. Faraday's idea was to try and share with ordinary people the beauty, charm, and usefulness of science—a goal that is still important today.

At the same time, the lectures raised much needed income for the Royal Institution, as people willingly paid to come and listen to great scientists speaking about their work. Faraday himself gave over a hundred of these talks during his time at the Royal Institution.

The children's champion

Faraday felt that young people as well as adults should have the opportunity to hear about exciting science firsthand, so he introduced his famous Christmas lectures for children. These lectures brought out the very best in Faraday—he passed his enthusiasm and energy onto his young audience, and loved sharing the fun and wonder of science. Once, he threw a coal scuttle, fire tongs, and poker at the Royal Institution's huge **electromagnet** —and all these heavy objects flew through the air and stuck to it!

Into the future

The Christmas lectures for young people that Faraday introduced, and for many years delivered, are still thriving today. Every year, one of the foremost scientists of the day runs a course of six lectures that are given live and also televised.

Through the medium of television, the excitement and wonder of science can reach not hundreds but millions of children each year. Michael Faraday would be delighted to see his Christmas lectures still going strong.

The Work Goes On

As Michael Faraday settled into his job as director of the laboratory at the **Royal Institution,** many offers of other jobs came his way. He was so widely respected for his work, and admired both personally and as a lecturer and teacher, that many other institutions tried to persuade him to work for them. One of the most notable offers came around 1827, from the newly formed University of London. They offered him the position of professor of chemistry, with the freedom to build up the department of chemistry as he wished. But Faraday turned this offer down, as he did almost all others. He said that he was grateful to the Royal Institution for the help and support it had given him early in his career, and that he wished to remain there and do all he could to further its interests now that he had become famous.

Research and more research

Faraday still spent most of his time doing active research. Fascinated by everything and anything, he would set himself questions to answer, and conduct rigorous experiments. For example, some of the richer London homes were lit by gas made from coal and oils, such as whale oil, supplied in compressed form in special cylinders. Intrigued by the liquid residue left in the cylinders when they were empty of gas, Faraday set out to investigate the liquid: separating it out, purifying it, and analyzing it. One component had not been seen before—Faraday called it "bicarburet of hydrogen." This important **organic** chemical is now known as benzene.

A whale is an unlikely source of benzene! But the gas that Michael Faraday investigated, and that led him to the discovery of benzene, was formed by heating whale oil and storing the gas that was given off under pressure.

Faraday was also involved, although not very successfully, in some experiments to develop glass that would be particularly good for making lenses. But more and more, his mind turned back toward electricity and **electromagnetism,** and his other research was gradually laid aside.

Faraday remained loyal to the Royal Institution despite receiving offers of work from many other establishments, including the University of London.

Personal sadness

In these years of professional development, Michael and Sarah Faraday had to deal with one great personal sadness. It became increasingly apparent that they were not going to have any children of their own. Both of them loved the company of children and young people, so this news must have been difficult for them to accept. Sarah poured much of her maternal feeling into caring for her absent-minded husband, and they both played a major part in their wider families, with various nieces spending much of their childhoods with their beloved uncle and aunt.

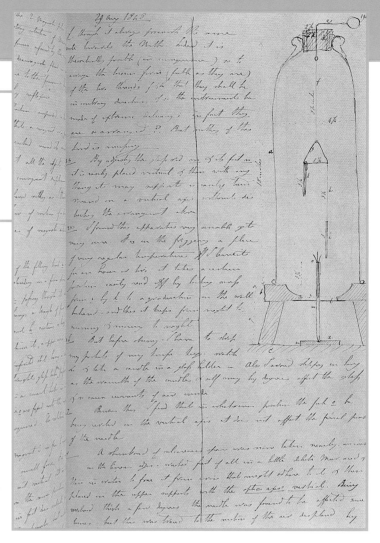

Faraday's simple **apparatus** was described in detail in his pages of carefully made notes.

Over the years, Faraday repeated the electrical and magnetic experiments performed by Oersted, Ampère, and others. He became convinced that just as electricity could produce magnetic effects, there must be a way to use magnetism to produce electricity. He became so determined to solve this problem that it became almost an obsession with him. Legend has it that he would always carry a small iron bar and a coil of wire in his pocket, so that if he had a spare moment, he could fiddle around and try to work out a solution.

The iron ring

Faraday made a soft iron ring and wound coil after coil of copper wire around it. He connected the wire to a **galvanometer,** which would measure any current that flowed, and then pushed a bar magnet into the ring. A quick "wave" of current was formed just as the magnet moved into the ring, and again as it moved out—but nothing happened while it was in the middle.

Making electricity

Finally, after days of frantic work, Faraday made his breakthrough. If pulsating currents could be made by pushing a magnet in and out of a **helix** of wire, would it be possible to create a steady current by using a constantly rotating movement? Faraday set up an apparatus in which a copper disk was rotated between the poles of a magnet, and wires attached to the edge of the wheel led any current generated to the galvanometer. To his dismay, when the wheel turned, the galvanometer moved only slightly. Faraday tried numerous arrangements of the leads until finally, by connecting one to the edge of the disk and one to the center, he recorded a weak but continuous deflection of the galvanometer. The deflection became larger as the wheel turned faster.

In two months of unbelievably intensive work, Michael Faraday had developed the **dynamo!** His discovery made the generation of electricity possible all over the world and changed society forever. But Faraday was never very interested in the practical applications of his work. He published his first results in 1831, and then, utterly exhausted by his efforts, he and Sarah took a well-earned break.

The iron ring on which Faraday experimented helped him discover a way to use magnetism to generate electricity.

The Transatlantic Rival

In the United States, Joseph Henry was trying to find a way to use magnetism to generate electricity about the same time as Faraday did his experiments in England.

Michael Faraday was, first and foremost, a **theoretical** scientist. This means he carried out his research and worked on his ideas for the pleasure of understanding how things worked. Once a problem was solved, he had little real interest in how the science he had discovered might be applied in everyday life. However, on the other side of the Atlantic, another inspired young scientist was working in the same area of electricity and magnetism—and he was of a much more practical frame of mind.

Joseph Henry

Joseph Henry (1797–1878) was born and raised in Albany, New York, where he studied and gained his first professorship in 1826. He was appointed professor of natural philosophy at the College of New Jersey (now Princeton University) in 1832. Like Faraday, he was fascinated by the relationship between electricity and magnetism, and he developed some of the most powerful electromagnets of his time. This work of Henry's almost certainly affected Faraday's thinking. Henry actually discovered the principle of **electromagnetic induction** several months before Faraday produced his first **dynamo.** But Henry had been criticized for using other people's ideas, just as Faraday had been. Still hurt by this criticism, Henry held back from publishing any more results, giving Faraday the time to reach the same conclusions and make his findings public. Thus, it is Faraday who is usually credited with the discovery of electromagnetic induction and the dynamo, rather than his counterpart in the U.S.

The telegraph meant that news, information about weather conditions, and cries for help could all be sent and received far faster than ever before. This changed the way society was run.

Theory and practice

The differences between the two men became very obvious as their careers progressed. Faraday continued to investigate the theoretical basis of physics, while Henry became very involved in the practical applications of what he had discovered. He greatly increased the lifting power and efficiency of electromagnets, making them useful in industry. He designed a new and better electric motor, and, most importantly, in 1831, he developed a primitive **telegraph** system using **electromagnetism.** This led eventually to the invention of the telephone. At the beginning of the nineteenth century, messages took days or weeks to cross a country or continent. By the end of the century, the same messages could be sent almost instantaneously by telegraph.

In 1846, Henry was elected secretary of the newly formed Smithsonian Institution. In this role, he set up research efforts in many areas of science. He was the first to organize **meteorological** studies and to use the telegraph to transmit daily weather reports—work that led to the formation of the United States Weather Bureau, now called the National Weather Service. Henry used his mind in a very different way than did Faraday, producing practical solutions to problems. Both were great men, however, and extraordinary thinkers for their time.

Faraday's Laws

Around 1820, a major controversy broke out. It had been noticed that if an electric current flowed through water, two gases—hydrogen and oxygen—were produced. This observation raised many questions. Theories abounded among the great scientists of the day, but none of them held up when tested, and none of them was right! In 1832, Michael Faraday joined the hunt and began to apply his mind to the observations that had been made. He worked by passing electricity through acidified water. The conclusions he had reached by the end of 1833 completely revolutionized the way **electrolysis** was understood, and built the foundations for all our modern understanding of the science.

Electrolysis

In electrolysis, electricity passes through a substance called an **electrolyte,** which can be a solution (with water) or a solid or molten material. Tiny particles carrying different charges are attracted to either the positive or the negative **electrode.** At these electrodes, they either lose or gain **electrons** to form stable **atoms** or **molecules.**

Not only did Michael Faraday explain what was happening during electrolysis, he also created and introduced the terminology—electrolysis, electrolyte, electrode—that we still use today.

Faraday's understanding of electrolysis shed light on a subject that was puzzling many of the great minds of the day.

This man works in the modern electrolysis industry. Today, electrolysis provides us not only with useful objects such as aluminum foil, but also with things simply to enjoy, like silver- and gold-plated jewelry.

Faraday's laws

As part of his careful work on electrolysis, Faraday measured the amounts of different substances given off during the process. As a result of all his observations and measurements, he formulated two laws that can be used to predict the outcome of any type of electrolysis. They are known as Faraday's laws, and they are still in use.

Into the future

Electrolysis is a common process in industry today. Aluminum, one of the most widely used metals, is extracted from its ore by electrolysis; so are fluorine and sodium. Copper is refined by electrolysis, and brine is split to form sodium hydroxide, chlorine, and hydrogen. Processes such as plating with silver, gold, or copper all use the same method of electrolysis. The calculations needed for all these processes still rely on Faraday's laws.

In Faraday's words:

Faraday's first law states: *"The quantity of a substance deposited, evolved, or dissolved at an electrode during electrolysis is directly proportional to the quantity of electricity passed through the electrolyte.'"*

Faraday's second law states: *"The quantities of different substances deposited, evolved, or dissolved at electrodes by the passage of the same quantity of electricity are directly proportional to the combining weights of the substances."*

33

Illness Strikes

In 1831, Faraday gave up much of his well-paid consulting work because he was determined to focus his energies on his work with **electrolysis.** This meant giving up more than half his yearly income, a difference that had a marked effect on the standard of living that he and Sarah could enjoy. As **Sandemanians,** they gave little thought to this, but friends and colleagues felt strongly that the government should award him a **pension** in recognition of his work. In 1835, after a brief disagreement with government officials, this pension was finally granted and accepted. However, at around the same time and after several years of very concentrated work, Michael's health failed dramatically.

The end of a career?

The first sign that something was wrong was when Faraday began to suffer dizzy spells and, even more frightening, complete lapses of memory. He had to cut down his work time more and more, until eventually he reluctantly listened to his doctors and took a complete nine-month break with Sarah in Switzerland.

When Faraday returned to England, he did no more work at all for several years; then he began to do research again only at a very slow pace.

In 1840, while his health was still fragile, Faraday was made an elder of the Sandemanian Church. This position involved giving sermons, carrying out services, and supporting other members of the church community. Sarah and Michael Faraday were well-known for their openheartedness and generosity to their friends, their families, and their church. At the same time, though, there were troubles in the church about the way teachings were interpreted, which Faraday found very stressful. The troubles ended in 1844, when Faraday, his father-in-law, brother, sister, and about fifteen other Sandemanians were excluded from the Church. This brought Faraday to a very low point indeed, but when he was restored to the fellowship a few weeks later, he picked himself up and began a remarkable recovery.

Much of Faraday's recovery and his continued ability to work was the result of the devoted care and protection given to him by his beloved wife, Sarah.

Back in harness

From 1845 on, Faraday's health recovered almost miraculously, to the point where he could once again immerse himself in his beloved science. He was able to conduct another seventeen years of brilliant research in his laboratory, although his memory was never again as good. He wrote himself pages of notes to make sure he could remember what he was doing, making it possible for him to continue as a respected and successful scientist.

The End of an Era

During the 1850s, Michael Faraday continued to work. He was offered many honors during these later years, including the presidency of the **Royal Society.** He was offered it once, refused, and then was asked again later, but he still declined. He was also offered a knighthood but did not accept it. He turned all these honors down because they did not fit with the beliefs of his **Sandemanian** faith or his own humble personality.

The memory fades

It became increasingly obvious that Faraday's glory days were over. His memory, which had given him trouble for years, was frequently letting him down. Although Faraday had regained his physical strength after his earlier illness, his mind—and especially his memory—was never the same again. He could remember the past but not the present. He dared not work in the same areas of research as other people, because he could not remember what they had done and feared he might again appear to steal ideas.

In 1857, a group of Royal Society members invited Faraday (second from left) to become president. He refused because of his poor health and his religious beliefs.

As Michael Faraday aged, he became incapable of scientific research, because the shining light of his brilliant mind was overshadowed by memory loss and other mental problems.

In 1861, Faraday retired, with great sadness, from his post as lecturer at his beloved **Royal Institution,** although he remained superintendent of the laboratories. In 1864, he gave up his role as an elder of the Sandemanian Church, and finally, in 1865, he retired from all his remaining positions. He and Sarah moved from the Royal Institution to a house in Hampton Court, which was provided by Queen Victoria herself in recognition of his achievements.

Fading light

From 1865 on, Faraday deteriorated rapidly. Toward the end of his life, he was rarely lucid, and was unable to do anything for himself, spending most of his time sitting in a chair staring vacantly into space. He was cared for lovingly by the ever-devoted Sarah and their nieces. Finally, on August 25, 1867, Michael Faraday died, still sitting quietly in his chair—although the great scientist's spark had been lost long before his heart ceased to beat.

Faraday could have had a grand funeral with burial in Westminster Abbey, but his funeral was in keeping with his Sandemanian faith. Michael Faraday was laid to rest in Highgate Cemetery after a very plain, private ceremony, and his headstone reads simply:

Michael Faraday
Born 22 September 1791
Died 25 August 1867

In Faraday's words:

"My memory wearies me greatly in working; for I cannot remember from day to day the conclusions I come to… I do not remember the order of things, or even the facts themselves."

Focus on Faraday

*Faraday spent his scientific life almost entirely at the **Royal Institution**. It has preserved much of his original **apparatus** and notes as a tribute to one of its most famous members.*

Michael Faraday was a scientist whose work spanned a great variety of disciplines. He made enormous contributions to chemistry, to the study of **electromagnetism,** to the understanding of the nature of electricity, and to **electrochemistry.** His work led later to the development of an area of physics known as **field theory.** His work covered light, gravity, glass, and steel along the way.

Faraday the genius

The impact of Michael Faraday's work was recognized and honored by his peers in his own lifetime. He never had to struggle to make ends meet, battling against hostile fellow workers. He made a living from his science right from the beginning, and earned enough throughout his life to live the way he chose. Fellow scientists respected and admired his work, even if at times the admiration was tinged with envy. Faraday had a remarkable gift of focus—he would wait until a problem had baffled many of his peers, and then apply himself to it with obsessive vigor until he came up with the solution. It must have been discouraging at times to be one of the many others who came close, but lost out to Faraday's genius. He was even awarded the ultimate accolade—he had a unit of electrical current named after him. The amount of electricity needed to release approximately one **mole** of any substance at an **electrode** is a **faraday.**

Faraday the educator

Faraday made his mark on the society in which he lived in another way, too. More than anyone else before him, he worked to encourage the public understanding of science. His Friday evening talks and the Christmas lectures for young people had an enormous impact during his lifetime, and continue to do so long after his death. There are few scientists who have done so much to involve and interest other people in the subject that they study.

Michael Faraday loved to think about problems just for the pleasure of solving them, not for their usefulness. His work has helped us discover more about many areas of physics, including electricity, of which this lightning is a beautiful example.

Faraday the theoretician

Another way in which Faraday differed from at least some of his contemporaries was in his attitude to his scientific work. He was interested in science for science's sake. He wanted to find out the answers to the questions that arose in his head for their own sake, so that he and others might better understand the beauty and order of the natural world. He had little interest in using the discoveries he made in a practical way—he left the applications to others.

Faraday's Legacy

Whatever the amount, wherever the place, the generation of electricity depends on the dynamo developed by Michael Faraday.

The work of Michael Faraday is fundamental to our modern understanding of electricity and magnetism. It has had an enormous effect on the modern world in a variety of ways. Perhaps one of the most important aspects of everyday life that is based on the theories of Michael Faraday is the generation, or production, of electricity. It does not matter whether the energy source for a power station is coal, oil, gas, or nuclear fuel; when it comes to generating electricity, the process depends on a **dynamo.** This is also true for wind power and wave power, however big or small the **generator,** or wherever in the world it is being used. Without the dynamo, the world would be a very different place. And while American scientist Joseph Henry and others developed the practical applications of the dynamo, it was Faraday who explored deeply into the theory of how and why it works.

A glimpse into the unknown

Modern particle physics is an area of academic study beyond the understanding of many of us. However, the **theoretical** exploration of the very nature of the matter that makes up our universe could yet yield secrets that will have enormous benefits for the human race. This branch of physics has its roots directly in the work that Faraday carried out on **field theory.**

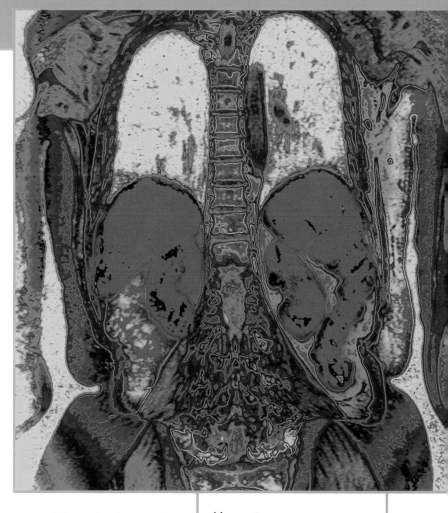

Magnetic resonance imaging is a part of the legacy of Michael Faraday that has a major impact on the health of people today. This scan shows the thorax and abdomen of a woman.

A much more practical legacy of Faraday's work is the use of magnetic resonance imaging (MRI) in the diagnosis of diseases such as cancer. This technique has moved Faraday's detailed work on magnetism and electricity right into the 21st century. It gives doctors a way of seeing clearly into the body without opening it up or damaging it in any way. X-rays were the first scientific tools that allowed us to do this, but their uses are limited. MRI scans of parts of the body give doctors sharp, detailed images of all the different tissues, and make the task of finding cancer in the body much easier. More than that, they can show the extent of a tumor precisely, making surgery and treatment increasingly accurate—and therefore much more effective. Faraday's legacy of scientific discovery will last for the foreseeable future, and will appear in many different areas of our lives. His was a rare talent.

This British stamp was produced in 1991—a true testament to Faraday's great and lasting legacy.

Michael Faraday began his life in the humble home of a **blacksmith.** He was raised in a family short of money but strong in the faith of their own **Sandemanian** Church. By the time he died, he was a figure of international renown, respected for his work in many areas of science—a man who had made his mark, not only on the age in which he lived, but on generations to come.

A life of dedication

Michael Faraday's first job was as an **apprentice** bookbinder. He did not continue with this career, but it gave him the opportunity to move into science.

From Faraday's arrival at the **Royal Institution,** his working life was dedicated to the pursuit of scientific knowledge. It is astonishing that one man could work on so many areas of chemistry and physics with such success. Faraday identified new **elements,** worked on stainless steel and optical glass, and made major breakthroughs in our understanding of electricity and **electromagnetism.** He discovered the principles of the first electric motor and the **dynamo,** which is fundamental to the generation of electricity. He unraveled the mysteries of **electrolysis,** determined the strength of current at the **electrodes,** and made the first steps into **field theory.** On top of this, he ran the Royal Institution and set up both the Friday evening talks and the Christmas lectures for young people. Michael Faraday was a man of genius.

Personal loyalties

In his private life, Michael Faraday was just as dedicated as he was in his work. His private dedication was to his beloved wife, Sarah, his family, and his church. Sarah and Michael were close partners all through their marriage, and although they were denied the joy of their own children, they took great delight in their nieces and nephews, and played a large part in these young people's lives. And to the Sandemanian Church—which was demanding, challenging, and exclusive—Michael Faraday gave total loyalty, even though at times the conflict between the beliefs of his church community and his work and the fame it brought him must have been very hard to deal with.

At the end of Faraday's life came the great sadness of the failing of his mind. It distressed his wife and family to see his struggle to remember the simplest things. What is hardest is to imagine how Faraday himself felt, being well aware of, and increasingly frustrated by, the deterioration of his mental powers. But nothing that occurred at the end of his life could dim the brilliance of the legacy he left behind—a legacy that still affects all our lives today.

Once Michael Faraday was given his first chance at the Royal Institution by the great Sir Humphry Davy, he never looked back.

Timeline

1698	A steam-powered pump is invented for use in mines.
1770	A steam-powered carriage is invented to pull heavy guns used for fighting on land. It is not successful because it is so difficult to steer.
1782	James Watt designs a steam system that can produce rotary movement.
1791	Michael Faraday is born on September 22.
1800	Alessandro Volta demonstrates the first battery.
1805	Michael is taken on as an **apprentice** bookbinder.
1812	Attends lectures given by the great scientist Sir Humphry Davy and decides to pursue a scientific career.
1813	Appointed laboratory assistant at the **Royal Institution;** later accompanies Davy on an expedition to Europe.
1815	Napoleon escapes from exile on the island of Elba.
1815–19	Michael Faraday gives lectures on chemistry to the City Philosophical Society.
1816	Faraday publishes his first paper.
1820	Hans Christian Oersted publishes a paper on **electromagnetism.**
1821	Faraday produces the first electric motor and is accused of stealing the ideas of William Wollaston. He marries Sarah Barnard on June 12.
1823	Publishes the results of his experiments with liquid **chlorine,** upsetting Humphry Davy.
1824	Elected a **fellow** of the **Royal Society.**
1825	Davy forgives Faraday and appoints him director of the laboratory at the Royal Institution.
1826	Faraday's Friday evening discourses at the Royal Institution become hugely popular.
1827	Faraday turns down an offer from the University of London to become professor of chemistry.
1831	Invents the **dynamo.** Joseph Henry demonstrates a primitive telegraph in the United States, based on the principle of electromagnetism.
1832	Faraday begins to study **electrolysis.**
1833	Faraday's laws on electrolysis are formulated.

1835	Begins to receive a **pension;** health begins to fail.
1837	Samuel Morse designs a telegraph that becomes widely used.
1840	Faraday is made an elder of the **Sandemanian** Church.
1841	Health problems force Faraday to abandon his work temporarily.
1844	Troubles in the church cause Faraday's exclusion and take a further toll on his health.
1845	Faraday is restored to the church and recovers his health.
1857	The **Royal Society** asks Faraday to be its president, but he refuses for health and religious reasons.
1864	Faraday gives up his role as elder of the Sandemanian Church.
1865	His mind failing, Faraday is unable to work any longer. He retires and spends the rest of his life at Hampton Court.
1867	Michael Faraday dies on August 25, at the age of 75.

More Books to Read

Gardner, Robert. *Electricity and Magnetism.* Brookfield, Conn.: Twenty-first Century Books, Inc., 1995.

Oxlade, Chris. *Electricity & Magnetism.* Chicago, Ill.: Heinemann Library, 2000.

Wood, Robert. *Electricity and Magnetism Fundamentals: Funtastic Science Activities for Kids.* Broomall, Penn.: Chelsea House Publishers, 1998.

Glossary

alchemy ancient "science" concerned with turning base metals into gold, and with finding the secret of eternal life

apothecary old name for a pharmacist

apparatus set of instruments for a particular task

apprentice someone bound to an employer for a set length of time to learn a trade or craft. This period of time is called an apprenticeship.

atom smallest particle of an element that still has all the element's properties

axis line around which a rotating body turns

blacksmith someone who works with iron, often making horseshoes and shoeing horses

chlorine element that exists as a gas at room temperature

dynamo machine for converting mechanical energy into electrical energy by the rotation of copper wire coils in a magnetic field

electrochemistry study of the links between electricity and chemistry

electrode conductor through which an electric current enters or leaves a battery

electrolysis breaking down of a chemical compound using electricity

electrolyte substance that conducts electricity when it is in solution or melted

electromagnetic induction production of an electric current using a magnetic field

electromagnetism magnetic field produced by an electric current

electron tiny negative particle that makes up part of the structure of an atom

element substance made up of only one type of atom

faraday amount of electricity needed to release one mole of any substance at an electrode

fellow member of a prestigious group, such as the Royal Society in England, where membership is usually by invitation only and based on contributions to a particular field

field theory theory explaining the way in which objects not in contact can influence each other

French Revolution civil war in France, during which the monarchy was replaced by a republic

galvanometer device used to detect and measure very small electric currents

generator machine for making electrical energy from mechanical energy. Generators can burn fuel or use the power of water, nuclear, wind, or solar energy.

helix spiral

indelible not able to be removed or erased

iodine element in the same chemical family as chlorine

meteorological dealing with the study of weather and climate

mews street or court lined with stables and carriage garages

mole amount of any substance that contains approximately 6×10^{23} particles

molecule very small unit of a particular substance, usually made up of more than one atom joined together

momentum mass times velocity

Napoleonic Empire French empire ruled by the Emperor Napoleon from 1804–1815

organic relating to living organisms such as animals and plants

pension money paid to someone to support them during retirement

quandary state of uncertainty

Royal Institution scientific body for research and teaching founded in England in 1799. The building in which the business of the Institution takes place is also known as the Royal Institution.

Royal Society most highly regarded academic group in Britain

Sandemanians small religious sect named after Robert Sandeman

smithy place where a blacksmith works

telegraph communications tool that works by sending electrical signals in code through wires

theoretical dealing with theories, or the abstract ideas and principles behind science, rather than practical application

velocity measure of the speed and direction of an object

Index